Nancy V. Lee

WHY ARE AMERICANS LIKE THAT?

Why Are Americans Like That?

A Visitor's Guide to American Cultural Values and Expectations

Stan Nussbaum

Illustrated by Kathleen Webb

Stan Nussbaum

*enculturation
books*

Published by Enculturation Books, Colorado Springs, Colorado, U.S.A.

For permissions email info@enculturation.org or write to Enculturation Books, 1348 Lily Lake Drive, Colorado Springs, CO 80921.

Manufactured in the United States of America.

ISBN: 0-9769146-7-0

 enculturation books

To find out more about Enculturation Books, please visit our web site, www.enculturation.org. Orders may be placed on-line or by email to orders@enculturation.org.

Kathleen Webb, freelance cartoonist, may be contacted via her web site, www.billykat.com.

Cover design by Beau Driver, www.beaudriver.com.

This book is presented to

_____

on

_____

by

_____

Phone: _____

Email: _____

for Duop, Pamir, Thuok
and all my other Sudanese refugee friends as
they begin their American lives

Contents

Preface: Welcome to America

Cartoons: 11, 21, 25, 29, 43, 50, 65, 71, 78, 86.

Welcome to America

Whether you are an international student, a business traveler, an immigrant or a tourist,

Welcome to America!
May your time here be full of good things.
May your studies or your business go well.
May your American friends be many.
May this book help you live the American dream and avoid the American nightmare.

The better you understand Americans and their cultural values, the better chance you have of adjusting well, avoiding embarrassment, making friends, and succeeding in your study or getting a good job. This book will introduce you to American values by explaining 100 common American sayings and why we say them.

The aim of this book is not to try to convince you that our proverbs or our cultural values are better than yours. Like any other culture, ours has plenty of weaknesses and plenty of strengths. This book aims to describe our culture clearly so you can understand it. Then you can decide for yourself what you think of it and what to do about it. Several empty pages are provided at the back of the book for your notes.

If you are trying to improve your English, this book should help. It is written in fairly easy English, and explanations of the more difficult words are given at the bottom of each page.

The most helpful thing for your English and your understanding of Americans is conversation with Americans, and this book will make it easy for you to start interesting conversations. You will find about sixty "Ask an American" questions here. None of these will sound offensive to Americans, though some might not be appropriate to ask in your country.

In America, do not be afraid to say what you are thinking. This will probably seem strange to you if you are from Asia or Africa, but it really is the way we do things here. You can practice in a safe way by reading this book and then sending me your suggestions about ways to improve it. Email <improvements@enculturation.org>.

I will take your questions or criticisms as compliments, not insults, for two American reasons. First, we value time, and you are showing me respect by taking the time to send me your opinion. Second, you are helping me achieve my goal of making future editions of this book even more useful, and we value people who help us achieve our goals.

We are glad you have safely arrived in the USA and that you have got this book to help you adjust to American life. As we say in this country, "Enjoy!"

Stan Nussbaum
Colorado Springs, April 2005

Chapter One

Introduction: An Overview of Ten Key American Values[1]

Here are ten very common sayings that will help you understand ten key American cultural values[2]. I call them the "Ten Commandments of American Culture" even though they are not really "commandments." They have no religious or moral authority like the "Ten Commandments"[3] of the Bible do for Jews and Christians. However, if you break any of these "cultural commandments," many Americans might think you do not fit very well in America. This book will help you avoid the problem by learning to understand American expectations.

While you are learning about American values, some of your American friends may also want to learn about the values of your country. Please do discuss these things with us. If you can help us understand you better, you enrich our lives.

---

[1] **Ten key values** - these ten values summarize most of the themes to be explained in later chapters.

[2] **Cultural values** – what most Americans would consider right, good and normal.

[3] **Ten Commandments** – the rules for life believed to have been given by God to the Prophet Moses on Mt. Sinai over 3000 years ago. They are rules such as, do not make idols, respect your parents, do not kill and do not commit adultery.

Commandment 1. You can't argue with success. (Be a success.)

Success is probably the highest value in American life. It relates to many other characteristics of American life—individualism, freedom, goal-setting, progress, experimenting, social mobility, making money, pragmatism[4], and optimism[5].

Americans want to "make a success of themselves." This is the "American Dream" which has attracted millions of immigrants[6] and has been taught to generations of American children. Everyone wants to be a success at something. If you do not think that way, you may be considered a failure.

It is almost impossible to criticize success. For example, if an employee does something without properly consulting his supervisor, and as a result the company gets a big contract with a new customer, the employee will get much more praise than blame. The success of getting the new contract will seem far more important than the failure to consult a superior.

Sometimes people will even say cheating is justified if it brings success. Other people, however, may disagree.

See page 10 for more details about success, including a cartoon and some "Ask an American" questions.

---

[4] **Pragmatism** – doing what works to achieve your goal.

[5] **Optimism** – expecting good things to happen.

[6] **Immigrants** – people who moved to the United States from another country.

Commandment 2. Live and let live. (Be tolerant.)

Americans love freedom and privacy. In a way, that means we love to be left alone. We don't want anyone interfering in our affairs, giving us advice, or trying to run our lives. We want people to "stay off our backs," "stay out of our way," and "mind their own business."

Perhaps *Live and let live* should be listed as the first commandment of American culture, even more important than success. It means that no one should object to anyone else's way of living. If you like opera and I like country music, that is fine. If you want to get married and I want to live with someone without marrying her, that is fine too. Many Americans believe that neither of us should try to influence the other or object to the way the other lives.

If we are not tolerant of other people, we may damage their self-esteem[7]. To attack someone's self-esteem is to break one of the most basic rules of American life.

> *See page 20 for more details about tolerance and self-esteem, including a cartoon and some "Ask an American" questions.*

Commandment 3. Time flies when you're having fun. (Have lots of fun.)

Americans try to have as much fun as possible. Much of our fun comes through various

---

[7] **Self-esteem** – people's view of their own value as human beings.

kinds of entertainment, especially TV. But we also try to turn other activities into fun. Shopping is fun. Eating is fun, and in case it is not enough fun, we will put a playground inside the fast-food restaurant so the kids can have fun playing while the grown-ups have fun sitting and eating. Learning to read can be turned into fun, as the Sesame Street TV programs show. Americans look for careers that are fun (although not many succeed). Having fun is the major preoccupation[8] of youth, retired people, and many of those in between.

In most situations Americans are very time-conscious. However, we forget to watch the clock when we are having fun. That is why "time flies," that is, time seems to go by very quickly.

See page 23 for more details about fun, including a cartoon and some "Ask an American" questions.

✓ Commandment 4. Shop till you drop.

Many Americans (especially American women) shop as a form of recreation. Even if we are not shopping for anything in particular, we simply enjoy looking at all the options. We love the whole process of choosing what to buy and where to buy it. It is a major topic of social conversation. If you want to

---

[8] **Preoccupation** – something people think about all the time.

impress an American friend, convince him or her that you are a "smart shopper."[9]

The saying, *Shop till you drop,* is never used seriously as a command and yet it holds a serious meaning. We are perhaps the ultimate consumer society,[10] and this saying describes us so well that it could be our national motto.

See page 28 for more details about choices, including a cartoon and some "Ask an American" questions.

✓ Commandment 5. Just do it.

We are people of action. We do not like too much planning. That seems indecisive and perhaps a waste of time. We do not like rules and regulations that prevent action. We strongly dislike authority structures where people are expected to inform several other people before they do anything. We get an idea and we want to *just do it.*

Action is seen as the key to success. Action is more valuable than planning, checking regulations, or informing people.

See page 42 for more details about initiative, including a cartoon and some "Ask an American" questions about initiative.

---

[9] **Smart shopper** – someone who knows where an item can be bought most cheaply.

[10] **Consumer society** – a society in which buying and selling are the central activities of life and what you own is the main measure of your value.

Commandment 6. You are only young once. (Do whatever you can while you have the chance.)

This commandment ties together the themes of several other commandments—freedom, fun, initiative[11] and time. It is a command to enjoy life to the full, taking advantage of every opportunity that comes along. For example, this is why lots of university students flock to the Florida beaches for spring break but the 40-year-olds don't. Adult responsibilities and schedules put an end to the freedom of youth.

See page 49 for details about youth and age, including a cartoon and some "Ask an American" questions.

Commandment 7. Enough is enough. (Stand up for your rights.)

Human rights and dignity are so basic to American thinking that we assume everyone else must think the same way. This proverb implies the command, "Stand up for your rights." In the American Revolution, America as a nation said to Britain, *Enough is enough*, that is, "You have ruled us for long enough. It has to stop."

As we saw in Commandment 2, *Live and let live*, Americans do not want people interfering in their lives. When we sense interference, we push it away.

See page 64 for more details about justice, including a cartoon and some "Ask an American" questions.

---

[11] **Initiative** – doing something because you want to or decide to, not because you are told to or expected to.

Commandment 8. Rules are made to be broken. (Think for yourself.)

We obey rules most of the time, but we see rules as someone else's idea of how we should do things. We think the rule might have been meant for some other situation, not our situation now. Therefore we break it and do what we think is a better idea. This proverb implies the commandment, "Think for yourself in every situation. Do not just obey rules."

Though Americans say, *Rules are made to be broken*, we never say, "Laws are made to be broken." Laws are official "rules" and we proudly claim that in America, "No one is above the law."

See page 69 for more about rules, including a cartoon and some "Ask an American" questions.

Commandment 9. Time is money. (Don't waste time.)

We Americans are very time-conscious and very money-conscious. Many of us get paid by the hour for the work we do. We give the employer our time in order to get money.

The idea that *time is money* has gotten into our minds so deeply that it affects our whole lives. Wasting time is as bad as wasting money, so we schedule everything and we hurry everywhere. We often signal the end of a phone conversation or a meeting by saying, "Well, I don't want to take up any more of your time." If you really want to annoy[12] an American, sit down and start talking as if you have nothing

---

[12] **Annoy** – bother, make someone angry with you.

else to do for the rest of the day. You will be breaking the Ninth Commandment of American culture, "Don't waste time."

See page 77 for more details about time, including a cartoon and some "Ask an American" questions.

✓ Commandment 10. *God helps those who help themselves. (Work hard.)*

In a list of "Ten Commandments," one might expect that God would be mentioned in the first commandment rather than the last one. But in American culture, God actually does come at the end of the list. For most Americans, God is much less a concern than success, money and time. (There are many Americans who put God at the top of their personal list of priorities,[13] but they are a minority within American culture.)

God helps those who help themselves could mean, "God rewards people who work hard" or it could mean, "God doesn't really help anyone. Your success depends on you, not God." Either way, the proverb points to the same commandment, "Whether you believe in God or not, work as hard as you can." It is better to be independent than to depend on other people.

See page 84 for more details about God, including a cartoon and some "Ask an American" questions.

---

[13] **Priorities** – things that are important, often listed with the most important one first.

Chapter Two

The Top Priority
in American Life

The "American Dream" is a dream of individual success. That is the top priority for many of us. We know that the dream has come true for many "self-made" people. They have set their goals. Their hard work has paid off. The whole nation admires their achievements. This is especially true of highly successful people who came from ordinary or poor backgrounds, such as Henry Ford, Marilyn Monroe, Billy Graham, Oprah Winfrey and Michael Jordan.

Success stories like these inspire us all to try to make a success of ourselves. We dream big dreams. Children all over America are practicing basketball, imagining themselves as the next Michael Jordan. More than anything else in life, we Americans want our biography[1] to be a success story, and the bigger, the better.

Ask an American

Can you name two or three people you would consider very successful Americans? Why do Americans admire these people so much?

---

[1] **Biography** – the story of someone's life.

9

What kinds of things do Americans have in mind when they talk about "being a success in life"?

SUCCESS AS AN IDEAL

 1.   *(Commandment 1)[2] You can't argue with success.* Though you may tell someone they are doing something in a wrong way, you have to stop criticizing them if their method works.

2.   *Nothing succeeds like success.* Like money in a savings account, success seems to compound[3] itself. A person who has a small success expects it to be followed by a bigger one.

3.   *Go for it.* Go ahead and try to achieve your goal. Don't worry about failing.

Americans have been described as pragmatists, that is, people who care more about success than anything else. Another way of saying this is, *"You can't argue with success."* This is what we call the "First Commandment" (most basic principle) of American culture.

Since success is so important, we spend a lot of time and energy setting our goals. The goals help us focus our lives and measure our success. "Mission statements"[4] have become popular

---

[2] **Check mark** – this symbol marks each of the "Ten Commandments" that were explained in Chapter 1.

[3] **Compound** – multiply over and over.

[4] **Mission statements** – one-sentence summaries of an organizational goal.

in American business. Even schools and hospitals write "mission statements."

Very few of us sit down and write out a personal "mission statement" but we do constantly set goals for ourselves. They can be huge goals like a goal in life or very small goals like getting three errands finished by 10:00. We hold ourselves accountable to these goals. If we cannot achieve them as planned, we experience stress and frustration.

To understand any particular American, learn what his or her goals are. If you can help an American toward an important goal, you will be treated very well.

Ask an American

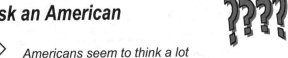

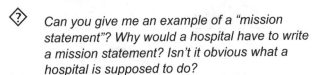

Americans seem to think a lot more about goals than we do in our country. What kinds of goals do you have for yourself this month or this year? Do you have goals for your whole life?

Can you give me an example of a "mission statement"? Why would a hospital have to write a mission statement? Isn't it obvious what a hospital is supposed to do?

Other proverbs about success

➤ *The end justifies the means.*
➤ *All is well that ends well.*
➤ *Killing two birds with one stone.*
➤ *All's fair in love and war.*
➤ *Always a day late and a dollar short.*

CARRYING OUT A STRATEGY

4. *There's many a slip between the cup and the lip.* This refers to a plan that has gone wrong. When one is drinking from a cup, one intends to get all the drink into the mouth, but this does not always happen. The plan is good but it can still fail.

5. *One thing at a time.* Concentration leads to success. The person who tries to do too many things at once may fail at all of them.

6. *When in Rome do as the Romans do.* Flexibility leads to success in unfamiliar circumstances. People may change their normal way of doing things in order to fit in better with those they are visiting.

7. *Don't put the cart before the horse.* Do things in a sensible order. For example, do something to impress your boss before you ask for a raise in pay. Don't ask for the raise first.

Once a goal is set, an appropriate strategy[5] may be chosen. This choice has to be made very carefully because a good strategy will bring success and a poor strategy may lead to failure.

A strategy has to combine the right amounts of many different values described in the proverbs. Some of these are concentration, flexibility and common sense. The wise person knows how much of each one is needed to bring success in each situation.

---

[5] **Strategy** – a careful plan for achieving a goal.

Ambition, self-confidence and hard work are required while a strategy is carried out. We will discuss these in later sections. Success such as winning the lottery[6] may be envied but it is not admired because it comes through sheer luck rather than strategy or effort.

Ask an American

 Suppose I wanted to live by the saying, "When in America, do as the Americans' do." What should I learn to do in an American way? What will help me fit in? What will make me look like a foreigner who does not fit?

Other proverbs about good or bad strategies

➤ *There is more here than meets the eye.*

➤ *Easy does it.*

➤ *Don't count your chickens before they are hatched.*

➤ *Flattery[7] will get you nowhere.*

TAKING RISKS CAUTIOUSLY

8. *Look before you leap.* Do not jump into a situation carelessly. You may land in difficulty.

---

[6] **Lottery** – a type of gambling run by the governments of some US states. A winner may receive a million dollars or more.

[7] **Flattery** – telling someone how wonderful she is even if you do not believe what you are saying. You only say it because you want the person to like you and give you something.

9. *Too good to be true.* This is often used to warn about advertising. An offer looks good but turns out to be misleading.

10. *There is no such thing as a free lunch.* Similar to the previous proverb. If someone you do not know offers you a free lunch or other gift, watch out. The gift may be a method of getting something from you.

11. *Time will tell.* Wait and see how something will work out. Do not trust a person or thing too much right now.

12. *Don't bite off more than you can chew.* Don't attempt something too large for you to handle.

Being great risk-takers, Americans have a lot of experience with strategies that go wrong. We have many proverbs that warn us about what to keep in mind when we take risks. *Look before you leap (8).* Realize that something that looks good might be *too good to be true (9).*

Risk-taking is usually admired but not if it is foolish. An overconfident[8] person may be warned, *Don't bite off more than you can chew (12).* Don't take an advanced chemistry course if you did not do well in the basic chemistry course.

Ask an American

   Can you give me an example of

---

[8] **Overconfident** – thinking you can do great things that you really cannot do.

a situation where you might say each of the following things: Look before you leap, There is no such thing as a free lunch, Time will tell.

Other proverbs about risks

➢ *Curiosity killed the cat.*
➢ *All that glitters is not gold.*
➢ *Seeing is believing.*
➢ *Where there's smoke there's fire.*
➢ *Better safe than sorry.*
➢ *Don't put all your eggs in one basket.*
➢ *A bird in the hand is worth two in the bush.*
➢ *Pride goes before a fall.*
➢ *Hindsight[9] is always 20/20.[10]*
➢ *The burned child shuns fire.*
➢ *Once bitten, twice shy.*

BEING CONFIDENT AND DETERMINED TO SUCCEED

13. *Where there's a will, there's a way.* Any problem can be solved if one is determined enough.

14. *So far so good.* Said by or to someone who is carrying out a plan taking one step at a time. Confidence increases with each step.

---

[9] **Hindsight** – looking back on a situation.

[10] **20/20** – proper, clear eyesight. The numbers are used by eye doctors to describe how clear or poor a person's vision is.

15. *Nobody bats a thousand.* No one succeeds all the time. Do not be discouraged by failures even if you have many of them. (The phrase comes from baseball where a batting average is calculated for each player, using 1000 to represent 100%. If a batter "got a hit" every time, his average would be "1000," but in fact the best batters usually average only between 300 and 350.)

16. *When the going gets tough, the tough get going.* When the situation is difficult, the determined people can handle it. They do not give up.

17. *If you can't beat 'em, join 'em.* If you cannot compete successfully with a person or group, stop competing and go join them. Then you can share in their success.

As we push for success, we think that almost anything is possible. We encourage each other to take risks. Perhaps this is because we are mostly people (or descendants[11] of people) who left the land of their forefathers and moved to America because it offered a better future for them and their children. That was a huge risk. For most Americans, that risk paid off. Today we are a nation of risk-takers—look how many of us put our money into the stock market!

Our confidence helps us handle the setbacks[12] that come with risks. We do not lose sight of

---

[11] **Descendants** – children, grandchildren, great-grandchildren and all the later people who can trace their family line back to the same person.

[12] **Setbacks** – events that "set you back," that is, things that push you farther away from your goal instead of bringing you closer to it.

our goal. We tell ourselves, *When the going gets tough, the tough get going (16).* Perhaps the set-back came because we did not make our first attempt in the best way. Perhaps the task was too big or the time was not right. We need to be patient and determined. We have to "hang in there."

Once in a while we do have to admit that we cannot achieve a goal, no matter which strategy we use. We give up on it, but we do not stop setting goals and seeking success. To us, that would be giving up on life and starting down the road to suicide,[13] the ultimate failure. Instead, we simply set a different goal and start looking for a strategy to succeed at that. We may even leave one group and join a different one in order to have a better chance of success the next time. *If you can't beat 'em, join 'em (17).*

Ask an American

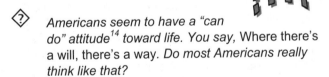

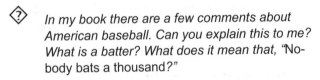

Americans seem to have a "can do" attitude[14] toward life. You say, Where there's a will, there's a way. *Do most Americans really think like that?*

In my book there are a few comments about American baseball. Can you explain this to me? What is a batter? What does it mean that, "Nobody bats a thousand?"

---

[13] **Suicide** – killing oneself.

[14] **"Can do" attitude** – confidence. The attitude that says, "I can do this."

How closely do you agree with this proverb: When the going gets tough, the tough get going*? Is that how you live your life?*

Other proverbs about determination

➢ *The sky is the limit.*
➢ *We'll cross that bridge when we come to it.*
➢ *Every little bit helps.*
➢ *If at first you don't succeed, try, try again.*
➢ *While there is life there is hope.*
➢ *It isn't over till the fat lady sings.*
➢ *Rome wasn't built in a day.*
➢ *There are other fish in the sea.*

Chapter Three

Self-esteem and Fun

Success is probably the top priority for most Americans, but self-esteem[1] and fun are valued almost as much. One cannot understand Americans without understanding these two things.

SELF-ESTEEM   THE DIGNITY OF THE INDIVIDUAL

18. *(Commandment 2) Live and let live.* Do not be judgmental. Do not try to control or punish other people. You live as you choose and let others live as they choose.

19. *Looking out for number one.* Protecting yourself carefully, even if you hurt others in the process. This is sometimes used to criticize a person who has abused or taken advantage of someone else, "All he was doing was looking out for number one." Or it may be used by a person to defend himself or herself, "There is nothing wrong with what I did. I was just looking out for number one."

20. *The customer is always right.* Businesses instruct their clerks not to do anything that might threaten a customer's self-esteem, no matter how unreasonable the customer is. Any complaint of any customer must be carefully and politely heard by any employee. The customer must not be made to feel ignorant.

---

[1] **Self-esteem** – your opinion of yourself.

20

Though there are far more proverbs about success than self-esteem, the few proverbs about self-esteem are crucial to American thinking. The three proverbs quoted above are the foundation for the American understanding of everything that is normal, good and right.

Americans think it is natural and healthy for every person to be *looking out for number one (19)*. From kindergarten[2] onward, schools and parents tell children how "special" each one is. Even if children do poorly in their schoolwork, teachers avoid giving them low or failing grades because that may damage their self-esteem, that is, their sense of self-worth. They will feel like failures, not successes. The philosophy of life is, "Express yourself," "Enjoy yourself," "Respect yourself," "Be true to yourself."

Like a desire for success, self-esteem can be seen as a core value of American culture. Self-esteem, which is closely related to personal dignity, is often seen as the most basic human right and the key mark of a psychologically healthy person. Nobody wants to have low self-esteem, and nobody wants to associate with people who do.

Whatever promotes self-esteem is good and whatever threatens it is bad. That is why racism, sexual harassment, child abuse, male chauvinism[3] and religious intolerance are so unacceptable in America today. They all attempt to assert one person's dignity or power in a way that tears down the dignity of others.

---

[2] **Kindergarten** – the first year of school, usually at age 5.

[3] **Male chauvinism** – the belief that men are more important than women.

This is also the reason that Americans like to be called by their first name rather than their title, except in special cases such as judges, doctors and the military. We do not want to make others feel inferior[4] to us since that would cause self-esteem problems for them.

Ask an American

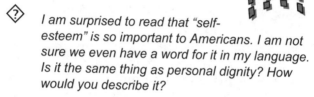

 I am surprised to read that "self-esteem" is so important to Americans. I am not sure we even have a word for it in my language. Is it the same thing as personal dignity? How would you describe it?

Can you tell me why your self-esteem is important to you? Is anything more important?

Is looking out for number one always a good thing? Is that how most Americans live?

Other proverbs about self-esteem

➢   *To each his own.*
➢   *Be true to yourself.*

See also: *Celebrate diversity (53).*

FUN

21. *(Commandment 3) Time flies when you are having fun.* A day seems short when it is full of enjoyable things but it

---

[4] **Inferior** – of lower quality or less importance.

seems like an eternity[5] if one is idle or stuck with a boring job.

22. *If it feels good, do it.* Live according to your desires at the moment. Forget about rules, regulations or consequences. Just have fun.

23. *Are we having fun yet?* This is a sarcastic[6] question. People who really are having fun do not have to ask such a thing. The question calls attention to the fact that something is not fun at all.

Some people build their whole lives around fun. They say, *If it feels good, do it (22).* Though most Americans do not go quite that far, we do spend a lot of time looking for ways to have more fun.

Weekend time is fun time. Families have fun together. On vacations people go wherever they will have the most fun. Sex is fun. New experiences are fun. Hobbies are fun. The people we like are the ones who are "fun to be with." We even say, "She's a fun person." We wish that our whole lives were fun, and they would be (we think) if we did not have to spend so much time working.

Americans are so individualistic that it seems that golf and tennis would be more fun for us than other sports. For some strange reason we love team sports in which everything depends upon each member of the group playing his or

---

[5] **Eternity** – an endless period of time.

[6] **Sarcastic** – containing a hidden insult.

her role in constant and perfect harmony with other team members. This is particularly true of American football and basketball.

We seem to recognize that, like success, fun is even more enjoyable when it is shared with other people. That may happen with a sports team, at a party, or just with a good friend, a husband or a wife.

Ask an American

⟨?⟩   *What do you do for fun?*

⟨?⟩   *Are you a fan of any professional sports team? Why do you like that sport and that team?*

⟨?⟩   *Who are your favorite friends to have fun with? What do you do together? If I asked to come along sometime, would you say, "The more the merrier[7]" or "Three is a crowd"?*

Other proverbs about fun

➤   *You only go around once in life.*
➤   *All work and no play makes Jack a dull boy.*
➤   *The more the merrier.*
➤   *It takes two to tango.[8]*

---

[7] **Merrier** – happier.

[8] **Tango** – a sexy dance.

CONFLICTS AMONG THE THREE PRIMARY GOALS

24. You can't have your cake and eat it too. Make up your mind. Sometimes one must choose between two very desirable things, giving up one in order to enjoy the other. If you have a piece of cake, you can save it to eat later. If you eat it now, you do not have it any more.

Individual success, self-esteem and fun may not be achievable at the same time. For example, success in a career may require such long working hours that the person has no time or energy left for fun. The person is a "workaholic."[9] On the other hand, if a student spends too much time having fun, he or she may flunk out[10] of college.

Success may also clash with self-esteem if the success comes through competition. Some educators have applied this to athletic games in grade school and prohibited[11] anyone from keeping score. The point of the game is not success but participation which builds self-esteem.

Self-esteem and fun may also conflict with each other. A bigger waistline means a smaller self-esteem, but dieting is never as much fun as eating.

---

[9] **Workaholic** – as an "alcoholic" is addicted to alcohol, a "workaholic" is addicted to work.

[10] **Flunk out** – fail so many courses that one is dismissed from school.

[11] **Prohibited** – made a rule against.

Ask an American

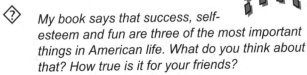

⟨?⟩ *My book says that success, self-esteem and fun are three of the most important things in American life. What do you think about that? How true is it for your friends?*

⟨?⟩ *Do you know many workaholics? Do you pity them, admire them or have some other attitude toward them?*

JUST THREE GOALS BUT THOUSANDS OF VARIATIONS

Success, self-esteem and fun are common cultural goals, but each American gets to choose his or her own definition of these things. For example, making lots of money may mean success to one person but not to another. Swimming may be fun for one person but boring for another. When we consider our choices, we love to have lots of options. This is true in every aspect of life.

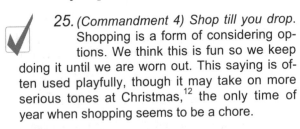

25. *(Commandment 4) Shop till you drop.* Shopping is a form of considering options. We think this is fun so we keep doing it until we are worn out. This saying is often used playfully, though it may take on more serious tones at Christmas,[12] the only time of year when shopping seems to be a chore.

---

[12] **Christmas** – December 25th, when Christians celebrate the birth of Jesus, the "Christ" (the King appointed by God). Americans commonly give gifts to friends and family on Christmas Day. American stores are busiest in December.

26. *Variety is the spice of life.* Variety is what makes life pleasurable. Boredom is seen as a threat and monotony[13] is the surest route to boredom.

Though there may be no proverb (yet) which says so, American life seems to go by the principle, "More choices mean a better life." The saying, *Variety is the spice of life (26)*, comes close to it, but spice is merely something nice. Life does not depend on spice. By contrast, choice is the "bread and butter" (the basic necessity) of American life.

Multiplication of options and choices is evident everywhere in America. There are 800 TV channels available on one satellite hook-up, hundreds of pictures and designs one can have imprinted on personal checks, dozens of flavors and types of dog food in the local grocery store, and a bewildering list of kinds of dressing you can have on your salad at the restaurant.

This is why we say, "*Shop till you drop.*" Shopping can be exhausting when there are so many things to choose from. The customer also gets used to the idea, "Some store somewhere has exactly what I am looking for (and maybe at a better price), so I won't buy this item which is almost right. I will keep looking." On we go to the next store.

Our desire for more choices is one of the main reasons more and more of us live in urban and suburban areas rather than small towns or rural areas. One has more choices in a city.

---

[13] **Monotony** – doing the same thing over and over.

Ask an American

Why is it so important to Americans to have lots of options to choose from?

If you were offered a job in a town of 1000 people, would you take it? Why or why not?

Other proverbs about variety

➤ *There is more than one way to skin a cat.*
➤ *One man's meat is another man's poison.*

Chapter Four

Ways to Achieve
Three Goals at Once

Of course we Americans would like to enjoy success, self-esteem and fun all at the same time with no conflict between them. We think we know at least three ways of achieving this—love, money, and playing to win. These are so important that some of us even value them for their own sake rather than as means to the three goals of success, self-esteem and fun.

LOVE

27. *Love conquers all.* Love overcomes all difficulties. For example, if a wife becomes crippled,[1] the husband's love conquers that problem. He continues to care for her and be faithful to her.

28. *Love finds a way.* Similar to previous proverb. Love is considered one of the most powerful and determined forces in the world. Two people in love will "find a way" to be together.

29. *Love makes the world go 'round.* Love is the driving force in all of life. Love makes life worth

---

[1] **Crippled** – unable to walk.

living. If you understand love, you understand everything about life.

Love and sex feature very largely in American culture because they represent an obvious way to achieve all three primary cultural goals at the same time—success, self-esteem and fun. Most Americans still see it as a success to have a steady, enjoyable love relationship, (and some men even think it is a "success" whenever a woman goes to bed with them). A person's self-esteem goes up when he or she is loved by someone desirable. And sex is fun, along with all the flirtations leading up to it. At least that is how it is in the movies.

You may get the impression from some Americans that the most important thing in life is to "fall in love," "be in love" and enjoy sex. Yet we Americans have big problems with love because we keep trying to mix it with our individualism. The mix usually does not work out the way we think it should.

That is why we have so many popular songs that say love lasts forever and so many other songs that wail about love that was betrayed,[2] abandoned or lost. We even have one song called, "The Greatest Love of All." It is not about love for a lover. It is about "learning to love yourself"! This is individualism gone wild.

Ask an American

---

[2] **Betrayed** – cheated on by someone you trusted. The person secretly breaks promises to you or helps your enemies.

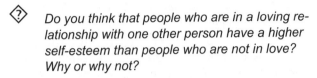

Do you think that people who are in a loving relationship with one other person have a higher
self-esteem than people who are not in love?
Why or why not?

Lots of American songs talk about love lasting
forever but lots of other songs talk about broken
hearts and lost loves. Which view is right? When
people fall in love, do they stop looking out for
number one *or not?*

Other proverbs about love

➤ *Love is blind.*
➤ *Absence makes the heart grow fonder.*
➤ *Out of sight, out of mind.*
➤ *Marry in haste and repent at leisure.*

MONEY

30. *Money talks.* Wealth has influence. People who
make big donations to political candidates are
"talking" to the candidates and expecting them to
listen.

31. *If you're so smart, why ain't you rich?* This question implies that intelligence will bring a person
money. It is used to insult an ordinary person
who has expressed an opinion as if it is the final
word on a subject.

32. *Money can't buy happiness.* This reminds people that money is not an ultimate value although
it often is treated as one. The saying may be
used as a comment when a wealthy but lonely
and wretched[3] person commits suicide.

---

[3] **Wretched** – deeply unhappy.

Money, like love and sex, is so important to Americans because it relates so closely to the three key values of success, self-esteem and fun. Money is a symbol of success and it can buy many other symbols. My self-esteem, as well as other people's view of me, will automatically increase if I have more money. Money buys the ticket to all kinds of fun. With money a person can reach all three main goals of American culture.

On the other hand, we say, *Money can't buy happiness.* We know this is true. We know that some wealthy people are miserable. Their misery tells us that there must be more to life than success, self-esteem and fun, and yet many of us keep chasing money anyway. We speak of "the almighty dollar" as if money were God. For many Americans it is a god. Some of us worship it, we make any sacrifice to get it, we hold it dearly and protect it zealously.[4] For such people, getting money is the center of life. It affects everything.

As we will see later, we have got used to thinking that *Time is money (86).* We think we should work longer hours in order to get more money, even though this reduces the amount of time we have for pleasure and family. When we say *Time is money,* we are almost saying, "Life is money" (though there is no such proverb).

---

[4] **Zealously** – eagerly and fiercely.

Ask an American

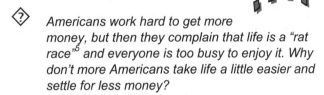

⟨?⟩ *Americans work hard to get more money, but then they complain that life is a "rat race"[5] and everyone is too busy to enjoy it. Why don't more Americans take life a little easier and settle for less money?*

⟨?⟩ *Suppose a good fairy[6] offered you this choice—for the rest of your life you can have all the love you need or all the money you need. Which would you take and why?*

Other proverbs about money

➢ *Beggars can't be choosers.*
➢ *The grass is always greener on the other side of the fence.*
➢ *Keeping up with the Joneses.*
➢ *Money isn't everything.*
➢ *The love of money is the root of all evil.*
➢ *A fool and his money are soon parted.*

PLAYING TO WIN

33. We're number one. This phrase means, "We are the best." It is often chanted[7] by the supporters of a sports team that has won a championship.

---

[5] **"Rat race"** – a meaningless but frantic competition.

[6] **Good fairy** – an imaginary being in children's stories.

[7] **Chanted** – shouted in rhythm together.

34. *Nice guys finish last.* If you are kind to your opponents, you will finish in last place in the contest. If you want to win, sometimes you may have to be unkind and impolite.

35. *Winning isn't everything.* One may enjoy the process of playing a game whether one wins or not. This traditional proverb is now often heard in the opposite form, *Winning isn't everything. It's the only thing.*

American play tends to be competitive[8] and oriented to achievement. For example, in Europe when people go hiking, most do it primarily to enjoy the walk or the hike. Americans do it because we want to conquer something or prove something that will build our self-esteem. Yes, we do have a bit of fun looking at nature as we hike, but a lot of the fun is in the achievement. Success gives us bragging rights.[9]

The same desire to conquer in play is obvious in the video games that American children love to play for hours on end. Even when we log onto the Internet, we do it with a "play to win" mentality.

And we do love the Internet. We have to. It is such an American thing. After all, it is instant, it is new and always changing, it is free (or almost free), it is fun, it is highly individualistic, it is private, it multiplies choices by the million, it lets us shop from home and it never threat-

---

[8] **Competitive** – eager to show that one can win.

[9] **Bragging rights** – the right to brag or boast about whatever we succeeded at doing.

ens our self-esteem unless we have to admit that we don't use it much.

Ask an American

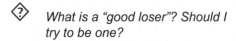 *What is a "good loser"? Should I try to be one?*

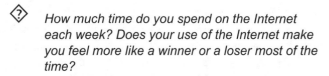 *How much time do you spend on the Internet each week? Does your use of the Internet make you feel more like a winner or a loser most of the time?*

Other proverbs about playing to win

➢ *It isn't whether you win or lose, it's how you play the game.*

➢ *The one who dies with the most toys wins.*

Chapter Five

Essentials for Achieving Any Goal

Americans assume two things about achieving any of our goals in life. First, each person must be free to pursue success. The purpose of government is to guarantee this freedom. Education and business are not supposed to create any barriers to this freedom. Second, each person must take initiative to use that freedom. In other words, government, business and education give us opportunities, but we have to make successes of ourselves.

FREEDOM   EQUAL OPPORTUNITY FOR ALL

36. *Life, liberty and the pursuit of happiness.* These three "inalienable[1] rights" of human beings were emphasized in the American Declaration of Independence in 1776. Liberty is the freedom to hold personal opinions, make personal choices and take part as the community elects its leaders and makes its choices.

37. *The land of the free and the home of the brave.* This concluding line from the national anthem

---

[1] **Inalienable** – something that no one can take away.

reminds Americans of freedom as our hallmark and bravery in war as the price of that freedom. The anthem was written after a battle in the War of 1812, when America defeated a British attempt to re-establish imperial control.

38. We shall overcome. This phrase is the title of a song which became a theme for African-Americans during the civil rights movement[2] of the 1960s. It referred to overcoming discrimination[3] and winning genuine freedom for minorities in America.

The "American Dream" of individual success depends on freedom for each and every citizen. When African-Americans, women, and other groups object to discrimination in education, housing, or employment, they are saying they have as much right to pursue the American Dream as anyone else does.

We claim that in America "all men are created equal" but we often treat minorities as "second-class citizens" and block their road to success. The civil rights movement and more recently the women's movement have pointed straight at the problem in many places. They sang, *We Shall Overcome*, and they really did overcome much of the discrimination in laws, policies, and personal behavior.

These protest movements were not challenging the core values of American culture. On the

---

[2] **Civil rights movement** – a citizens' campaign in the 1960s that changed many American laws and customs affecting ethnic minorities.

[3] **Discrimination** – unfair treatment based on race or gender.

contrary, they were affirming them. Protesters were demanding freedom to make successes of themselves. They were protesting a system in which their hard work was not rewarded fairly.

The American reaction to the attacks on September 11th shows that we believe these were intolerable attacks on our freedom. We all took the attacks personally because they affect our life goals personally. If thousands of the most successful people in the most successful corporations in America can be destroyed at their desks in a ball of fire, then what "successes" are the rest of us working for?

We have our goals and we insist on being free to pursue them. No attack by a foreign enemy or discrimination by anyone in our own country can be allowed to interfere in "the land of the free."

Ask an American

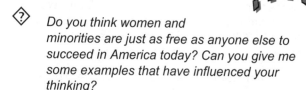

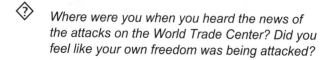

Do you think women and minorities are just as free as anyone else to succeed in America today? Can you give me some examples that have influenced your thinking?

Where were you when you heard the news of the attacks on the World Trade Center? Did you feel like your own freedom was being attacked?

PERSONAL INITIATIVE

Freedom is like a sports field. It has been cleared of other obstacles and activities so that people can play on it. But freedom can remain unused, just as a sports field can. By itself, freedom does not make anyone a success. Many American proverbs encourage people to take some initiative and use their freedom. In fact, there are so many proverbs about initiative that we have to break them into groups to deal with them.

Doing something is better than doing nothing.

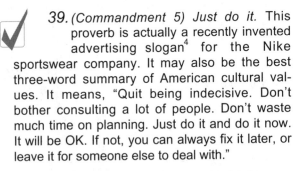

39. *(Commandment 5) Just do it.* This proverb is actually a recently invented advertising slogan[4] for the Nike sportswear company. It may also be the best three-word summary of American cultural values. It means, "Quit being indecisive. Don't bother consulting a lot of people. Don't waste much time on planning. Just do it and do it now. It will be OK. If not, you can always fix it later, or leave it for someone else to deal with."

40. *The best defense is a good offense.* Be pro-active[5] and goal-oriented, not timid or conservative. Aim to conquer, not merely to protect yourself.

---

[4] **Slogan** – a short statement describing a core value.

[5] **Pro-active** – ready to take action before the situation forces you to.

Americans are doers, and that means we achieve a lot in life. We do not accept bad situations as inevitable. We try to do something about them. We protest. We invent. We improve. We believe progress is possible and any individual can make it. We work hard without giving up, and we often succeed.

On the other hand, *Just do it (39)* is extremely bad advice in many other cultures. Americans who operate that way are very offensive when visiting other countries. Americans get a reputation for being impatient and inconsiderate. We do not consult the people who should be consulted before action is taken. We ask directly for whatever we want.

Ask an American

 When have you used the saying,
Just do it, *or when have you heard someone else use it?*

Other proverbs about taking initiative

➤ *Talk is cheap.*
➤ *Put your money where your mouth is.*
➤ *Actions speak louder than words.*
➤ *Never put off till tomorrow what you can do today.*
➤ *The road to hell is paved with good intentions.*
➤ *Idle hands are the devil's workshop.*

See also: *Opportunity only knocks once (88).*

Depending on yourself and your own initiative

41. *Stand on your own two feet.* Grow up; act like an adult. Don't ask me to do something for you. This may be said to a young or immature[6] person who depends too much on others. It is like a cow kicking a grown calf that still wants to suckle.

42. *If you want something done right, do it yourself.* This discourages people from trusting anyone except themselves. It may be said by someone who asks another person to do a job for him or her and then complains about how it was done.

43. *There is no harm in trying.* A person expects to be respected for making an effort even if it does not succeed. This view encourages people to take risks.

44. *No pain no gain.* One must put forth an effort in order to succeed. (This saying comes from physical fitness instructors. They say that if you do not exercise hard enough to make your muscles hurt, the exercise is not doing you much good.)

In America growing up means becoming independent, *standing on your own two feet (41).* Children are dependent on others. Adults are seen as independent and self-sufficient. This contrasts sharply with many traditional cultures where growing up means becoming interdependent with other adults. In those cultures

---

[6] **Immature** – not yet acting like an adult.

the main questions in life are, "Whom can I depend on?" and "Who is depending on me?" Americans do not take those questions very seriously. We just assume it is safer to depend on ourselves.

Americans believe success is better than failure but failure is better than not trying. When we fail we say, "At least I tried." We expect people to respect us for trying. We think they will forgive us easily if we tried in a wrong way as long as our intentions were good.

We do not expect this independent kind of life to be easy, but we say, *No pain, no gain (44)*. We are willing to go through some pain in order to achieve our goals. We look down on people who set no goals and only look for the easiest way to get through life.

Ask an American

? *You say,* If you want something done right, do it yourself. *In our country we would rather say, "If you want something right, get some friends to help you." Doesn't our way make more sense than the American way?*

? *In my country it is a great disgrace to fail, so we do not try things unless we are fairly sure we can succeed. But in America, you seem to try anything. Do you really think it is better to fail at something than not to try it?*

Other proverbs about depending on your own initiative

➤ *You've got to take the bull by the horns.*

➤ *Money doesn't grow on trees.*

➤ *Necessity is the mother of invention.*

➤ *Too many cooks spoil the broth.*

➤ *Easy come, easy go.*

➤ *Nothing ventured, nothing gained.*

➤ *First come, first served.*

Knowing the proper limits of initiative

45. *Give him an inch and he'll take a mile.* Be careful of presumptuous[7] people who take more initiative than they should. If you do people a small favor or delegate a little power to them, they may take advantage of you.

46. *If it ain't broke, don't fix it.* Do not bother trying to improve something if it is already working satisfactorily. That is a waste of time and you run the risk of breaking the thing while you are trying to improve it.

47. *All things come to him who waits.* Sometimes patience is better than initiative.

In most cases Americans like initiative but not always. These proverbs warn us about initiative of certain kinds.

Sometimes it is better to leave things alone than to try to improve them. Sometimes humility and

---

[7] **Presumptuous** – acting as if you have more permission than you have really been given.

patience may be the best route to success. However, we see these warnings as exceptions. In most cases we would rather take charge and try to make things happen as we want.

Ask an American

 I don't understand how Americans decide when to take initiative and when to leave things alone. You say, There is no harm in trying, *but you also say,* All things come to him who waits. *Can you explain this for me?*

Other proverbs about limits to initiative

➤ *Fools rush in where angels fear to tread.*
➤ *Leave well enough alone.*
➤ *The cure is worse than the disease.*
➤ *Count to ten before you lose your temper.*
See also: *Let a sleeping dog lie (80).*

Chapter Six

The American View
of Human Beings

AGE

48. *(Commandment 6) You are only young once.* Do what you can while you are young. For example, go to Europe for your whole summer break from college. Once you graduate from college and begin your adult working life, that opportunity will be gone.

49. *A man is only as old as he feels.* A person's energy level is more important than age.

50. *Oh, for the vigor[1] of youth again.* An expression used sadly by a middle-aged or older person, often when observing a child or youth doing something very active.

From an American point of view, youth is the ideal time of life. It is the time of the most freedom, the most choices, the most vitality and the fewest obligations. Middle age and old age are a long, losing battle to stay young, look young and feel young. That is why so much of the spam in America is advertising Viagra and Cialis. Aging is seen only as a loss of liveliness and strength, not an increase in prestige or wisdom.

---

[1] **Vigor** – energy and strength.

Retirement, usually beginning at age 65, is seen as a time of self-indulgence. Many retirees move south to Florida or Arizona because the weather is warmer, even though this may mean moving far away from relatives and friends.

People from other cultures may wonder whether retired Americans have any sense that they are worth anything as human beings. They are hundreds or thousands of miles from their children. No one shows them any special respect. But they still have their self-esteem. They may regard retirement itself as an achievement, perhaps the one great success to which the rest of life was looking forward. A retiree may say, "I worked all my life for it. I made money and saved money. Now I am free to have fun."

One of the most important differences between American culture and many others is that in America one's sense of worth comes more from personal achievements than from relationships. A great deal of American culture will not make sense to the outsider until this point is recognized.

Ask an American

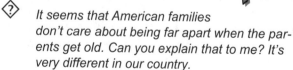

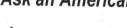 It seems that American families don't care about being far apart when the parents get old. Can you explain that to me? It's very different in our country.

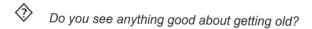 Do you see anything good about getting old?

Do you agree that "one's sense of worth comes more from personal achievements than from relationships"?

GENDER

51. *A man's home is his castle.* At home a man is like a king, completely free to do as he wishes.

52. *A man may work from sun to sun, but woman's work is never done.* Men may have to work long days but they can go home to rest in the evening. Women (working in the home or at an outside job or both) can never get away from what used to be called "woman's work," such as cooking and cleaning.

53. *Celebrate diversity.* A recent slogan intended to promote acceptance of people different from oneself. It is often used by the homosexual community. In that case it means, "Do not criticize anyone because of his or her sexual orientation.[3] Instead accept and even celebrate the fact that people have different likes and dislikes in sexual activity as in other aspects of life."

The definitions of male and female roles in American society are under fierce debate in America today. What makes a man masculine? What makes a woman feminine? How can a woman be fulfilled as a housewife if there is no obvious personal achievement and no pay? Is

---

[3] **Sexual orientation** – ones preference for sexual relationships with the opposite sex, the same sex or both.

sexual orientation purely a matter of personal preference?

Because Americans are so divided about gender issues,[4] most of the above proverbs about gender will offend somebody. For example, feminists are offended by sayings like, *A man's home is his castle (51)*, or *Woman's work is never done (52)*. They believe these are old-fashioned, oppressive ideas.

Traditionalists, on the other hand, are deeply offended when homosexuals adopt the new slogan, *Celebrate diversity (53)*. Traditionalists see homosexuality as perversity,[5] not just diversity, and they do not want anyone to celebrate perversity.

Ask an American

⟨?⟩ *Do you agree with the slogan,*
     Celebrate diversity*? Why or why not?*

⟨?⟩ *Do women have a different place in American society than they did ten or twenty years ago? What has changed and what else still needs to change (if anything)?*

Other proverbs about gender

➢ *Clothes make the man.*

---

[4] **Gender issues** – issues about male and female identity.

[5] **Perversity** – gross immorality; human beings acting like animals.

> ➢ *Beauty is only skin deep.*
> ➢ *It's a woman's prerogative[6] to change her mind.*

HUMAN NATURE

54. *Nobody is perfect.* Everyone has shortcomings. This is used as an excuse for a minor mistake that has been made.

55. *Boys will be boys.* People will act according to their nature, including some mischief.[7] This is sometimes used to describe irresponsible but not too seriously wrong behavior by men. In other words, grown men will sometimes act like little boys.

56. *One bad apple can spoil the whole barrel.* Do not associate with bad people. They may spoil you as a rotting apple spoils the apples next to it in the barrel.

Americans recognize that all human beings have faults. *Nobody is perfect (54).* We can keep a healthy self-esteem without thinking we are perfect. But we could not keep it if we thought we were basically evil.

We tend to think that only a very few people are really bad people. They are the "*bad apples*" *(56)* who influence ordinary people to do bad things. They deliberately harm people and may even enjoy watching others suffer. The

---

[6] **Prerogative** – a right that cannot be questioned.

[7] **Mischief** – behavior that is wrong but not very serious.

rest of us don't do that so we don't see ourselves as evil.

If we happen to hurt someone while we are only intending to protect ourselves, we call that "self-defense" or *Looking out for number one (19)*. If we do something and someone is offended by it, we may excuse ourselves by saying, "That's just the way I am," or *Boys will be boys (55)*. We call this "self-expression."

This may not make much sense to foreigners. Americans consider selfishness to be very bad but self-interest (including self-esteem, self-sufficiency, self-defense and self-expression) to be very good.

Ask an American

◇⟨?⟩ *Americans seem to see a big difference between selfishness and self-interest, but aren't those two things very similar? What do you think the difference is?*

◇⟨?⟩ *Would you agree that most Americans are basically focused on themselves but not basically evil?*

Other proverbs about human nature

➤ *To err is human.*
➤ *When the cat's away the mice will play.*
➤ *Better the devil you know than the devil you don't.*

Chapter Seven

Loyalties, Groups and Families

LOYALTIES

57. *If you scratch my back, I'll scratch yours.* If you do a favor for me, I will do one for you. (This refers to a pleasurable back-scratch, not an attack from behind.)

58. *A friend in need is a friend indeed.* My true friend is the one who shows loyalty to me by helping me when I am in need.

59. *Rats desert a sinking ship.* A losing cause is abandoned. This is generally used to criticize the people who are abandoning a project that appears to be failing, since they are compared to rats.

60. *A good captain goes down with his ship.* Contrast to previous proverb. The captain remains on board his ship even when all hope to save it is lost.

As we have seen in various other sections of this book, Americans' primary loyalty is to ourselves as individuals. The proverb *Looking out for number one (19)* sums up this view. All other duties and loyalties have to be seen in light of this basic loyalty to self.

This means that a person's loyalty can never be assumed. It must be earned by continually showing the person that he or she will be better off by remaining loyal. For example, a sports team that wants loyal fans[1] must keep winning. Even marriage partners may feel they have to keep earning each other's loyalty.

Loyalty may break down if a cause seems lost. *Rats desert a sinking ship (59),* that is, saving one's own life is more important than the welfare of the cause or the group. On the other hand, we also say, *A good captain goes down with his ship (60).* He is so loyal to the ship that if she ever begins to sink, he does everything he can to save her and everyone on board. He may even give up his life as he is doing his duty.

We admire that kind of heroic loyalty, but we rarely see it or do it. Loyalty to companies, to neighborhoods and even to friends seems to mean less than it did in the past. Loyalty puts limits on our freedom to choose, and we generally do not like those limits.

Ask an American

⟨?⟩ *What loyalties do you have besides loyalty to yourself? How much have those loyalties been tested?*

⟨?⟩ *Is there any person or group of people you expect to be loyal to you for your whole life, no matter what happens? Why will they be loyal?*

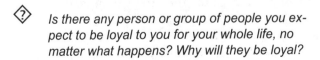

---

[1] **Fans** – supporters of a sports team.

Other proverbs about loyalties

➢ *One good turn deserves another.*

➢ *A live dog is better than a dead lion.*

➢ *My country, right or wrong.*

➢ *Blood is thicker than water.*

➢ *No man can serve two masters.*

➢ *A dog is a man's best friend.*

GROUPS

61. *Birds of a feather flock together.* People with similar characteristics and interests will spend their time together. This may be used as a warning against associating with bad people. Others will assume one is like them.

62. *There is safety in numbers.* Do not take large risks all by yourself. Do not walk alone on a dangerous street at night.

63. *Many hands make light work.* Cooperation makes a job much easier.

64. *Misery loves company.* When things go badly, a person wants a group of friends to share the pain. This can also mean that when people are miserable, they may want to make others miserable too. Such people can be dangerous.

One might suppose that Americans are so individualistic that we have little use at all for belonging to any group. This is not quite true. We have already seen that belonging to a group can make fun more enjoyable and success more likely. *Many hands make light work (63).*

Belonging to a group may also be important because of shared interests *(Birds of a feather flock together, 61)*, safety *(There is safety in numbers, 62)*, and sympathy *(Misery loves company, 64)*.

Americans do not mind group relationships. What bothers us is group obligations.[2] We join groups easily and we leave groups easily. In other words, we join groups which serve our personal interests and we remain with a group for as long as we wish to enjoy it, but no longer. Americans' ease with group relationships makes it easy for us to engage in conversation or form casual friendships with complete strangers but more difficult for us to form deep and lasting relationships. Personal freedom or self-development is rarely sacrificed for the sake of a group.

This may be changing. Today many American youth see their parents as lonely, stressed out, empty people who do not belong to any group that means anything to them. Not wanting to be like their parents, they are attaching more importance to personal relationships in small groups.

Whether we are old or young, our wealth makes it hard for us to develop any group solidarity.[3] The American way of life is set up to

---

[2] **Obligations** – what the group expects or requires of all members.

[3] **Solidarity** – a strong feeling of belonging. Willingness to sacrifice for the benefit of the group.

prevent difficult times or, if they come, to allow us to deal with them on our own. But this also prevents us from developing strong bonds in our groups. We never find out who our real friends are.

Ask an American

◇ *Do you agree that "Americans enjoy groups but don't like group obligations"? What do you think that says about Americans?*

◇ *What groups do you belong to that are an important part of your life? How long have you belonged to them?*

Other proverbs about groups

➢ *Two heads are better than one.*
➢ *A house divided against itself cannot stand.*
➢ *Two is company and three is a crowd.*

See also: *One bad apple can spoil the whole barrel (56).*

THE FAMILY AS A GROUP

65. *Charity begins at home.* One should be kind to close relatives before doing good to the community in general.

66. *Home, sweet home.* Traditionally used on plaques hung on the wall, this phrase reminds people of the ideal home. It should be a place of warmth, love and joy. The phrase may be used by people returning home at the end of a long trip.

67. Home is where the heart is. Home is wherever ones loved ones are. The size or appearance of a house does not make it a home or keep it from being a home.

The very first point to recognize in a discussion of American families is that Americans apply the word "family" almost entirely to the "nuclear family"[4] not to the "extended family" as in most other cultures. Many Americans live hundreds or thousands of miles from their nearest "extended family" relative. Contacts with aunts, uncles and cousins are often lost. Many of us do not have any one city we really call "home." We do not have a family cemetery.[5] Our parents or grandparents do not live in our home.

The proverbs about home reflect the era of my parents' childhood much more than the situation today. *Home, sweet home (66)* sounds like wishful thinking to a lot of us today. Things are different now. Home is not where the heart is. Home is where the television is (though again, we have no proverb that says so, and most Americans may laugh at that phrase.)

---

[4] **Nuclear family** – only parents and children living together while the children grow up. The "extended family" means other relatives such as grandparents, adult brothers and sisters, cousins, etc.

[5] **Cemetery** – place where the dead are buried.

Everything about American homes is moving toward greater individualism. Each family member goes off to her own room and her own TV or computer. The microwave oven splits up the family so a family rarely eats a meal at the same time.

There is much talk in America about a recovery of "family values."[6] A popular religious movement in the 90s called "Promise Keepers" filled football stadiums nationwide for weekend all-male conferences. Men were urged to keep their promises to wives, children and God. The problem with such a campaign is that just like other loyalties and group relationships, "family values" put limits on individual choices and freedoms. Not all Americans want to pay that price in order to improve family relationships.

If we want to recover strong family relationships, our proverbs will not help us much. Unlike many other cultures, American culture has no common proverbs specifically about being a good parent, husband, wife or child, or about showing special respect to a person in any of these roles.

Ask an American

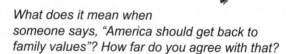

 What does it mean when someone says, "America should get back to family values"? How far do you agree with that?

---

[6] **Family values** – beliefs that emphasize the importance of family relationships.

How many cousins, aunts and uncles do you have? When did you last see them?

Other proverbs about the family

➢ *There is no place like home.*
➢ *Baseball, motherhood and apple pie.*
➢ *Like father, like son.*
➢ *Spare the rod and spoil the child.*

Chapter Eight

Fairness, Blame and Conflict

JUSTICE AND FAIRNESS

In any culture which places such a high value on individual success won by strategy, hard work and wise risk-taking, one has to ask what is considered fair. Are there any moral limits to strategy? How are success and freedom limited by justice?

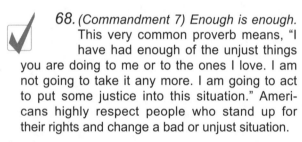

68. *(Commandment 7) Enough is enough.* This very common proverb means, "I have had enough of the unjust things you are doing to me or to the ones I love. I am not going to take it any more. I am going to act to put some justice into this situation." Americans highly respect people who stand up for their rights and change a bad or unjust situation.

69. *What goes around comes around.* What you do to others, especially if it is bad, will eventually be done to you. As you seek your own success, do not treat other people badly. They may take revenge[1] and spoil your success.

70. *Do unto others as you would have them do to you.* Similar to previous proverb (which could be stated, "Do not do to others what you do not want them to do back to you.") The "Do unto others"

---

[1] **Take revenge** – try to get even. Attack the one who attacked you.

> form is the "Golden Rule" from the Bible. It is not
> a warning but a command—treat others justly.

71. *Innocent until proven guilty.* In a court of law, the
    accused person is presumed innocent at the
    start. The burden of proof[2] always rests on the
    accuser, not the accused. The jury will not con-
    vict the person unless the proof is clear.

Human rights are the standard of American
justice. Whatever protects human rights is
just; whatever goes against human rights is
unjust. Every American of whatever status has
many personal rights, guaranteed by the "Bill
of Rights" in the Constitution. These include
such things as the right to speak one's mind in
public (even if this insults the government), the
right to worship as one pleases and the right to
trial by a jury of fellow citizens.

When people's rights are violated,[3] they are expected to react strongly enough to stop the injustice. Sometimes it may also be considered
fair for them to require some payment for the
injustice that was done to them or even to in-
flict a punishment. *What goes around comes
around (69).*

Since Americans believe that all human beings
have the right to be treated fairly, we will not
let anyone treat us unfairly. Such treatment
shows that the person thinks we are slaves,
animals or some other thing that is less than a
human being. We will not stand for it.

---

[2] **Burden of proof** – responsibility to prove something.

[3] **Violated** – broken without a legal reason.

Ask an American

<?> *When did something bother you
so much that you said to yourself,* Enough is
enough*? What did you do to change it?*

Other proverbs about justice and fairness

➤ *Silence is consent.*

➤ *Turnabout is fair play.*

➤ *Honesty is the best policy.*

➤ *Justice is blind.*

➤ *Finders keepers, losers weepers.*

➤ *Possession is nine-tenths of the law*

See also: *If you scratch my back, I'll scratch yours
(57); Don't get mad, get even (84).*

BLAME

72. The devil made me do it. I am not to blame for
what I did. I could not help it. Some power outside of me was forcing me to act in that way.

73. If the shoe fits, wear it. If an accusation is true,
accept the blame. (This saying can also mean,
"If a suitable opportunity comes to you, take it.")

74. You made the bed, you lie in it. You created a
certain situation so you are now responsible to
take the consequences.

75. *The pot calling the kettle[4] black.* Since the pot and the kettle are equally black from the cooking fire, the pot has no right to criticize the kettle. This might be used if someone who gossips[5] criticizes someone else for gossiping.

76. *Get a life.* Do not be so unreasonably critical about tiny things. Find something better to do with your time.

If we succeed at something, we want to take credit for it. If we fail, we want to find someone else to blame. We may playfully say, *"The devil made me do it (72)."* This is an excuse used by people who know they have done something wrong but want to avoid the penalty. It does not necessarily mean they really believe a devil exists or has any influence over their choices.

By passing the blame we try to protect our self-esteem. Several proverbs remind us that each individual really is responsible for her actions. *You made the bed, you lie in it (74).* Justice means that a person will have to pay for his crimes. No individual can escape this responsibility before the law of the land, regardless of personal status, wealth, or power.

Though we do not like to take responsibility for our own actions, we love to demand that other people take responsibility for theirs. If their action hurts us in any way, we make them pay.

---

[4] **Kettle** – a large old-fashioned cooking pot.

[5] **Gossips** – spreads stories, often not exactly true, that harm other people.

Americans sue[6] (and win) over matters that would get laughed out of court in most countries.

Ask an American

Why do Americans say, *"The devil made me do it,"* if they don't believe there is a devil?

What do you do to protect yourself from being sued? Have you ever been sued or considered suing someone else? What was the problem?

Other proverbs about blame

➤ *You can lead a horse to water, but you can't make him drink.*

➤ *Crime does not pay.*

➤ *Be sure your sins will find you out.*

➤ *Chickens come home to roost.*

➤ *There are two sides to every story.*

AUTHORITIES AND RULES

When freedom of choice, self-development, self-esteem and self-expression are core values in a culture, there is not much room left for authorities and rules. We have already seen several proverbs that imply that each individual is his

---

[6] **Sue** (or "file suit") – go to court to accuse another person of harming you in some way and ask the court to force the person to pay for the harm done.

or her own authority. *If it feels good, do it (22)*; *Just do it (39)*; *Live and let live* (18) and *The customer is always right* (20). There are also proverbs that directly mention authorities and rules.

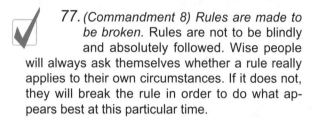

77. *(Commandment 8) Rules are made to be broken.* Rules are not to be blindly and absolutely followed. Wise people will always ask themselves whether a rule really applies to their own circumstances. If it does not, they will break the rule in order to do what appears best at this particular time.

78. *The voice of the people is the voice of God.* The ultimate authority in a society is found in the consensus[7] of ordinary people.

79. *Power corrupts.* Do not trust a person who has been in power for very long. When people are put into positions of power, they gradually forget what life is like for ordinary people. They become more likely to abuse their power, perhaps without even realizing it.

In many cultures, proverbs remind people to trust and respect authorities of all kinds. By contrast, American proverbs teach people to question and challenge authorities. Our nation was born in a revolution that threw off an unwanted authority, and we have been throwing off authority ever since. Many of us do not want to deny all authority by saying, *If it feels good, do it (22)*. Yet we each want to be our own authority with as little limitation as possible from other authorities in government, society, family and the workplace.

---

[7] **Consensus** – community agreement after discussion.

If an authority makes a demand on us, we want to know the reason. If the reason does not look obvious and necessary to us, we may say, *Rules are made to be broken (77)*. For example, if a child asks a parent, "Why can't I do that?" and the parent replies, "Because I said so," the child might not accept this. If the parent does not give a convincing explanation, the child might not obey. Many children think that authority lies in the reason, not in the parent.

American skepticism[8] about authorities is also true of rules. Most Americans see rules as limits to freedom. The fewer rules the better.

In fact, we do not like to quote proverbs in a way that makes them sound like rules. Sometimes we may stand a proverb on its head[9] to show we do not accept it as a rule any more. For example, the old saying, *Winning isn't everything (35)* becomes *Winning isn't everything, it's the only thing. Crime doesn't pay* becomes *Crime pays.* Or we change *Flattery will get you nowhere* to *Flattery will get you everywhere.* The person who can question authority is more respected than the one who submits to authority without thinking.

Ask an American

 If American children are taught to question every authority including parents and

---

[8] **Skepticism** – doubt. Unwillingness to trust.

[9] **Stand a proverb on its head** – change a proverb to the opposite meaning.

teachers, when and how do they learn to accept authority? How did you learn it?

 Americans say, Rules are made to be broken, *yet most of the time you obey rules. How do you decide which rules to keep and which ones to break?*

Other proverbs about authorities and rules

➢ *There is an exception to every rule.*
➢ *The exception proves the rule.*
➢ *The devil can quote scripture.*

CONFLICT AND RECONCILIATION

80. *Let a sleeping dog lie.* Do not meddle in something that will cause you no trouble if you leave it alone. If you wake up the "dog," it may bite you.

81. *If you can't stand the heat, get out of the kitchen.* Quit complaining. Withdraw from an activity if you do not like the conflict and criticism it brings. Let other people do it without you.

82. *Two wrongs don't make a right.* If someone does a wrong to you, react with justice, not by doing something vicious.[10]

83. *He who laughs last, laughs best.* If a person does wrong to someone and laughs at him or her, the victim will look for a way to get revenge. When revenge is taken, the victim *gets the last laugh,* defeating the other person.

---

[10] **Vicious** – intending to cause as much harm as possible.

84. *Don't get mad, get even.* Similar to the previous proverb. When someone treats you badly, do not just get angry, express your anger in action.

85. *Let bygones*[11] *be bygones.* Do not bring up an old problem. Pretend it never happened.

Americans do not enjoy conflict for its own sake. The proverb, *Let a sleeping dog lie,* advises people to avoid conflict if possible. Americans tend to avoid discussion of religion and politics because they believe such discussion can easily lead to conflicts. (University students are less worried about this than other Americans.)

We do realize that some degree of conflict is normal in life and may even be healthy. It helps people learn how to stand up for themselves, which is very important in an individualistic society. But we are disturbed by the fact that conflict is getting more violent in our society.

For example, "road rage" is one of the most frightening new forms of violence. This term refers to one driver attacking or even killing another on the highway because of the way he was driving. The attacker thinks this way: "I am just as important as anyone on the road. That driver was acting like the whole road belongs to him. I had to show him that he cannot get away with that. *Enough is enough"* (68).

Though Americans believe in protecting our personal dignity and we may say, *Don't get*

---

[11] **Bygones** – things that have "gone by," that is, things that are over and should be forgotten.

mad, get even, we are not at all sympathetic[12] to this kind of violence. We don't want self-assertion to get out of hand. That is why *Live and let live* (Commandment 2) is such an important proverb for us. It sets limits on aggressiveness.[13] There is also a gentler side to American values that says, *Let bygones be bygones (85).*

Ask an American

❓ *Do you generally avoid talking about religion and politics in order to avoid conflict with other people? Can you explain that for me? People in my country love to argue about those things.*

❓ *How do you explain road rage? Does it indicate anything about America in general or is it only a few crazy people doing it?*

Other proverbs on conflict and reconciliation

➤ *It takes two to make a quarrel.*
➤ *The pen is mightier than the sword.*
➤ *People who live in glass houses should not throw stones.*
➤ *Sticks and stones may break my bones but words will never hurt me.*
➤ *Opposites attract.*
➤ *Revenge is sweet.*

---

[12] **Sympathetic** – willing to understand.

[13] **Aggressiveness** – a tendency to force oneself on others.

> ➤ *Forgive and forget.*
> ➤ *Time heals all wounds.*
> ➤ **See also:** *Boys will be boys (55).*

Chapter Nine

Time and Change

If you get the impression that Americans are always in a hurry, you are right. Americans look at time as a scarce, valuable thing. There may be more American sayings about time than any other subject, and they are probably the sayings you will hear the most.

 86. (Commandment 9) Time is money. Time can be converted to money, that is, wages are often paid per hour of work. Managers want employees to do things quickly because "time is money." If employees waste time, the company loses money.

87. Making every minute count. Doing something productive all the time. Not letting any time "slip away."

88. Opportunity only knocks once. Similar to previous two proverbs. Opportunity is like an unexpected stranger passing by. It knocks on someone's door. If the person fails to answer the door, opportunity goes away and knocks on someone else's door. It does not return to the same person.

89. The sooner the better. A call for quick action or quick change. Once a decision has been made, there is no point in waiting to carry it out.

90. Make it short and sweet. Speak briefly and to the point. We do not have time for the details.

In chapter 4 we noted the connection between time and money. Life is seen as an hourglass in which the days slip by like grains of sand until one's time is up. Life is not seen as an accumulation,[1] an unfolding, a growth. It is a race, a race against time, and the human being always loses.

What is true of a lifetime is also true of each day, hour and minute. Americans are time-conscious to an extreme. The watch is our worst slave driver.[2] This view of time accounts for the very high level of stress in American life today.

Since time is limited and lost opportunities are gone forever, one has to go through life *making every minute count (87).* That means one is always busy doing something (work or play) or experiencing something.

We schedule everything, including our play. Then we say our schedules are so full that we need a vacation, but even on a "vacation" we try to pack in as many experiences as we can. We joke about getting home and having to recover from our vacation.

Time spent sitting and reflecting does not count for much. It doesn't make any money. It doesn't "do" anything. In fact, silence makes Americans nervous, as if we think time is being wasted or boredom is on the way. We try to fill up the silence, perhaps by turning on a radio or TV just to have some noise in the background.

---

[1] **Accumulation** – a gradually growing collection.

[2] **Slave driver** – a thing or person that forces us to do what we do not want to do, as if we were slaves.

Ask an American

?   *Americans seem to be obsessed with time,* making every minute count. *How does that attitude improve the quality of life and how does it reduce it?*

?   *Do most Americans think they are too busy? If so, how did they get that way? Why do they stay that way?*

?   *My book says that Americans do not think that sitting and reflecting on life is very important. Do you agree? When do you sit in silence and reflect? What do you think about?*

Other proverbs about time

➢   *Time's a-wasting.*
➢   *Time flies.*
➢   *No time like the present.*
➢   *Now or never.*
➢   *Make hay while the sun shines.*
➢   *He who hesitates is lost.*
➢   *Business and pleasure don't mix.*
➢   *The early bird catches the worm.*
➢   *Early to bed and early to rise makes a man healthy, wealthy and wise.*
➢   *Haste makes waste.*
➢   *Better late than never.*

See also: *You are only young once (48).*

Change and progress

91. *Time marches on.* Time is marching to its own steady drumbeat. It does not slow down or stop for anyone.

92. *A new broom sweeps clean.* A new person in power will change many things and improve the situation. Change is better than leaving things as they are.

93. *Tomorrow is another day,* (or, *Tomorrow is a new day*.) No matter how bad things are right now, a person may hope for better prospects in the morning. New opportunities will come.

94. *History repeats itself.* There are patterns in history. Nations rise and fall for similar reasons. Nations do not change their ways or learn from the mistakes of others. They repeat them.

We live in a society where everything can change, and almost everything does. There are new styles of clothing, new hit songs, maybe a new job or even a new spouse. We elect a new president. We open a new highway, a new mall and a new housing development. We expect all this change as *Time marches on (91).*

Many changeless traditions common in other countries are rare or absent in America. There is no American national costume, no definitive American folk tales or myths, few folk songs that everyone knows and no standard American way to conduct weddings or funerals. We do not even have an official national language.

We welcome change because we have a deep belief that *Tomorrow is another day (93),* and things are going to get better. Someone will find a cure for AIDS, a cheaper alternative for gasoline or a diet pill[3] that works. The human beings of the future will be stronger, smarter, and happier than people today.

What is the basis for our faith in progress? Historically it has been faith in individual hard work and bright ideas, especially in the areas of science and technology. For example, we point to the computer as an idea that has brought huge changes, mostly good, to many parts of life.

As much as we like change, we know that some things are almost impossible to change. For example, we doubt that our government will ever do anything efficiently. Government is by nature bureaucratic,[4] monopolistic[5] and non-profit. Nevertheless, we keep trying to "change the system," "re-invent government," etc. We try for small changes even when we despair about any big changes.

Ask an American

What are the biggest changes you have made in your life?

My country has lots of traditions and they give our lives meaning. Traditions do not seem to be very important in America, and I don't quite

---

[3] **Diet pill** – a pill that causes a person to lose weight.

[4] **Bureaucratic** – organized in a very structured way.

[5] **Monopolistic** – not allowing any competition.

understand where American life gets its mean-
ing without them. Can you help me?

⟨?⟩   *Is the world generally changing for the better or*
going downhill?[6] Will technology make life much
better for most people in the next generation?

⟨?⟩   *You say, "History repeats itself." Does that mean*
it is a waste of time to try to change things?

Other proverbs about change

➤   *The worm turns.*
➤   *Here today, gone tomorrow.*
➤   *The darkest hour is just before the dawn.*
➤   *Will wonders never cease?*
➤   *You can't teach an old dog new tricks.*
➤   *The more things change, the more they stay the*
same.
➤   *Nature abhors a vacuum.*
➤   *The leopard cannot change his spots.*
See also: *Time and tide wait for no man (100).*

---

[6] **Going downhill** – getting worse.

Chapter Ten

Hope and God

OPTIMISM

In chapter 2 on success we saw that Americans take risks confidently and work with determination in spite of setbacks. In chapter 9 we saw the American belief that changes are usually improvements. This optimism is also clear in the following more general proverbs.

95. *Look on the bright side.* Try to see the good side of a difficult situation. Keep your hopes up.

96. *Half a loaf is better than no bread at all.* Sometimes we will not be able to get all we want or hope for. At such times of only partial success, we should be glad for what we do get.

These proverbs represent a basic American cultural belief that we should be positive about life, even the parts of life that seem difficult. If we *look on the bright side (95)*, we are more likely to keep trying for success. Though we never like to settle for a partial success, *Half a loaf is better than no bread at all (96)*. Perhaps we can get the other half of the loaf later. We have almost limitless faith in our own ability to change things for the better.

Our optimism affects the way we look at the rest of the world. We have built a nation that has become the global center of economic and military power. We imagine, rightly or wrongly,

that if our influence could become even
stronger throughout the world, the effect would
be good for everyone, not just for us. Oppressive[1] rulers would be replaced by responsible
ones. Civil wars would stop. Women would be
treated with dignity. Poverty would decline. On
the other hand, if nations do not welcome
American influence and American values, we
are not optimistic about their futures.

Ask an American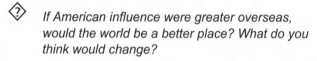

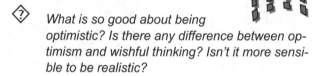 *What is so good about being
optimistic? Is there any difference between op-
timism and wishful thinking? Isn't it more sensible to be realistic?*

*If American influence were greater overseas,
would the world be a better place? What do you
think would change?*

Other proverbs about optimism

➢ *Every cloud has a silver lining.*
➢ *No news is good news.*
➢ *Lightning never strikes twice in the same place.*

UNSEEN POWERS; DESTINY

 97. *(Commandment 10) God helps those
who help themselves.* God looks favora-
bly on people who take initiative. If you
want something, work for it.

---

[1] **Oppressive** – using power unjustly.

98. *In God we trust.* This motto is clearly displayed on every American coin and bill. It means many different things to different Americans.

99. *God bless America.* This prayer is also the title of a song often sung on patriotic occasions. Sometimes politicians use it as the final line in a speech, especially when the issue is war.

100. *Time and tide wait for no man.* When something's time has come, it will happen and nothing can stop it. It is like an ocean tide coming in to the shore.

In many parts of the world, America is seen as a "Christian country." By comparison with most European countries, America is indeed very religious. Nevertheless we have no common proverbs that describe the greatness of God or instruct people to respect God. God is barely mentioned in our proverbs and when he is, he gets little credit for anything.

For example, we say, *God helps those who help themselves (97).* This can mean either that God will bless those who take initiative or that God is not a factor in how things turn out. The idea is that if one merely sits and prays but takes no actions, nothing good will happen.

It may appear that in America the real "god" (the ultimate center of attention and devotion) is the individual. Even many of the religious Americans try to get God to revolve around us, rather than adjusting our lives to revolve around God. We want God to meet our individual needs. We are not so interested in fitting into any divine master plan for the universe. The vast majority of us Americans say we believe in God but, to put it crudely, we often act as if God is to be used not worshipped.

We have a few proverbs about impersonal forces such as destiny, fate or history. We may say, *Time and tide wait for no man (100),* but these sayings are far outweighed by our proverbs on individual initiative. Americans want to believe that anything is possible through individual effort. We do not believe that fate, God, or any other unseen power has determined things and left us powerless to change them.

Ask an American

?> *When you say,* God helps those who help themselves, *does that mean that you believe God really does help them or you don't believe God does anything, so people had better do things for themselves?*

?> *Why does American money say, "In God we trust"? What does that mean to you?*

?> *Why was "God Bless America" sung so much after the World Trade Center was destroyed? Did Americans think about God any more or any differently after that attack?*

?> *My book says, "It may appear that the real 'god' in America is the individual person." What do you think that means? How true do you think it is?*

Other proverbs about unseen powers

➢ *Marriages are made in heaven.*

➢ *What will be will be.*

> ➤ *The good die young.*
> ➤ *Man proposes, God disposes.*
> ➤ *You can't fool Mother Nature.*

See also: *The devil made me do it (72); History repeats itself (94).*

Conclusion

Like all cultures, American culture has some great strengths, some glaring weaknesses and some strange paradoxes. It may be too simplistic[1] to conclude that Americans are lonely super-achievers, but there is some truth to that. We try to get everything without giving up anything, but it seems *you can't have your cake and eat it too (24)*.

Success, self-esteem and fun appear to be the most highly valued things in our culture. Love, money and "playing to win" are valued nearly as highly. Personal freedom and personal initiative make it possible for Americans to pursue these values.

While we are *looking out for number one (19)*, we give less attention to group loyalty, family relationships and sexual morality. All these tend to put limits on the individual pursuit of the primary values. As for God and fate, they get some attention but when they conflict with core cultural values, the core values usually take priority.

American culture is changing rapidly in areas such as gender roles, where there is no agreement about what is proper and desirable. It is

---

[1] **Simplistic** – explaining something only on the surface without really understanding it.

hard to know what the next generation will do with the culture they inherit. It seems that they may be less achievement-oriented and more people-oriented than their parents. They certainly have more options, more money, more free time, and more teaching on self-esteem than any previous generation. How can it be that so many of them are still bored, aimless and taking drugs? *If we're so rich, why ain't we smart? (contrast 31)*.

American culture assumes that if a society creates opportunities for its youth, everything else will turn out right. That assumption is not standing up well. America has not yet determined what else it needs or where else it should look. If America changes this basic assumption, the effects will spread through the whole culture and transform it, but in what direction? We do not know. We cannot find direction in sayings like *Just do it (39)* or *Go for it (3)*. They don't even tell us what "it" is.

America has vast wealth, power and influence. It may be the best country in the world for shopping, having fun, or making your life a success. But is it the best country for "living"? Are we the freest people in the world and yet voluntary slaves to the clock and the credit card? Is consumerism the key to the good life or the start of the rat race? Is the whole American Dream *Too good to be true? (9) Time will tell (11)*.

Alphabetical List of Proverbs

The numbers in the following list refer to the number of the proverb, not the number of the page on which it is found.

A friend in need is a friend indeed. 58
A good captain goes down with his ship. 60
A man is only as old as he feels. 49
A man may work from sun to sun, but woman's work is never done. 52
A man's home is his castle. 51
A new broom sweeps clean. 92
All things come to him who waits. 47
Are we having fun yet? 23

Birds of a feather flock together. 61
Boys will be boys. 55

Celebrate diversity. 53
Charity begins at home. 65

Do unto others as you would have them do to you. 70
Don't bite off more than you can chew. 12
Don't get mad, get even. 84
Don't put the cart before the horse. 7

Enough is enough (Commandment 7). 68

Get a life. 76
Give him an inch and he'll take a mile. 45
Go for it. 3
God bless America. 99
God helps those who help themselves (Commandment 10). 97

Half a loaf is better than no bread at all. 96
He who laughs last, laughs best. 83

History repeats itself. 94
Home is where the heart is. 67
Home, sweet home. 66

If it ain't broke, don't fix it. 46
If it feels good, do it. 22
If the shoe fits, wear it. 73
If you can't stand the heat, get out of the kitchen. 81
If you can't beat 'em, join 'em. 17
If you scratch my back, I'll scratch yours. 57
If you want something done right, do it yourself. 42
If you're so smart, why ain't you rich? 31
In God we trust. 98
Innocent until proven guilty. 71

Just do it (Commandment 5). 39

Let a sleeping dog lie. 80
Let bygones be bygones. 85
Life, liberty and the pursuit of happiness. 36
Live and let live (Commandment 2). 18
Look before you leap. 8
Look on the bright side. 95
Looking out for number one. 19
Love conquers all. 27
Love finds a way. 28
Love makes the world go 'round. 29

Make it short and sweet. 90
Making every minute count. 87
Many hands make light work. 63
Misery loves company. 64
Money can't buy happiness. 32
Money talks. 30

Nice guys finish last. 34
No pain no gain. 44
Nobody bats 1000. 15

Variety is the spice of life. 26

We shall overcome. 38
We're number one. 33
What goes around comes around. 69
When in Rome do as the Romans do. 6
When the going gets tough, the tough get going. 16
Where there's a will, there's a way. 13
Winning isn't everything. 35

You are only young once (Commandment 6). 48
You can't argue with success (Commandment 1). 1
You can't have your cake and eat it too. 24
You made the bed, you lie in it. 74

Further Reading

An expanded edition of this book is being published in fall 2005 by Orbis Books under the title, *American Cultural Baggage: How to Recognize and Deal With It.* That version is designed to

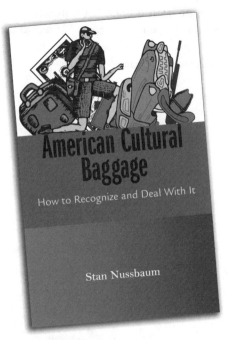

help Americans become aware of their own culture before they go to work or live elsewhere. Then they are more likely to appreciate and adjust to other cultures instead of misunderstanding and clashing with them. For a fuller description see www.orbisbooks.com.

Another helpful book similar in size and simplicity to *Why Are Americans Like That?* is Sarah Lanier's work, *Foreign to Familiar: A Guide to Understanding Hot- and Cold-Climate Cultures.* It is available from McDougal Publishing, www.mcdougalpublishing.com.

For those who want to dig deeper into the subject, useful books like *Living in the USA (6th ed.)*, *American Ways: A Guide for Foreigners in the United States (2nd ed.)*, and many others are available on the web site of Intercultural Press, www.interculturalpress.com.

The Author

Dr. Stan Nussbaum has been involved in cultural and religious research and training since 1977. Besides living in Lesotho (southern Africa) and England for seven years each, he has taught in many countries such as India, Korea, Malaysia, Kenya, Ghana and Lithuania. Currently he is coordinating a seven-country research program on the grass roots response of Christian congregations to the HIV/AIDS crisis.

He has long held a special interest in proverbs as windows into a culture. He initiated and co-ordinated the African Proverbs Project, a four-year pan-African project funded by a research grant from The Pew Charitable Trusts. The Project's work, including over 28,000 African proverbs and several volumes of related studies, is compiled in a CD, *The Wisdom of African Proverbs*, available from his current employer, GMI Research Services, www.gmi.org.

Americans have a proverb, "Will it play in Peoria?" It means, "Will ordinary Americans like it?" Peoria is a middle-sized city in central Illinois, which is in the Midwest, and its people are considered typical of Americans. Stan Nussbaum grew up six miles from Peoria in Morton, a town of 15,000, where his parents and one of his sisters still live. He is the father of two and grandfather of two. Since 1993 he and his wife Lorri have made their home in Colorado Springs.

Notes

Page	

Notes

Page	

Notes

Page

Notes

Page	

Notes

Page

Notes

Page

Notes

Page	

Notes

Page

Notes

Page	

Notes

Page

Notes

Page	

Notes

Page

Notes

Page	
Page	

Notes

Page